*Quick*GUIDES
everything you need to know...fast

Choosing and Using Consultants

by John Baguley

reviewed by Frank Opray

WIREMILL
PUBLISHING LTD

Across the world the organizations and institutions that fundraise to finance their work are referred to in many different ways. They are charities, non-profits or not-for-profit organizations, non-governmental organizations (NGOs), voluntary organizations, academic institutions, agencies, etc. For ease of reading, we have used the term Nonprofit Organization, Organization or NPO as an umbrella term throughout the *Quick*Guide series. We have also used the spellings and punctuation used by the author.

Published by
Wiremill Publishing Ltd.
Edenbridge, Kent TN8 5PS, UK
info@wiremillpublishing.com
www.wiremillpublishing.com
www.quickguidesonline.com

British Library Cataloguing in Publication Data
A catalogue record for this book is available from the British Library.

ISBN Number 1-905053-26-6

Printed by Rhythm Consolidated Berhad, Malaysia
Cover Design by Jennie de Lima and Edward Way
Design by Colin Woodman

Disclaimer of Liability
The author, reviewer and publisher shall have neither liability nor responsibility to any person or entity with respect to any loss or damage caused or alleged to be caused directly or indirectly by the information contained in this book. While the book is as accurate as possible, there may be errors, omissions or inaccuracies.

CONTENTS

INTRODUCTION

There are a hundred types of consultants and a thousand ways they can help, but are they right for you and your organisation? Are they not going to be extortionately expensive and only tell you what you already know?

This Guide takes you through the consultancy process, and helps you decide how and when to bring in a consultant as well as how to make the most of their services, ensuring that you have value for money and that your organisation welcomes your initiative.

The first time I appreciated the value of a consultant was when I took up a new position as Director of Fundraising at a national organisation, where I discovered that a consultant had recently been hired to map the organisation's future fundraising. Her report containing a series of recommendations was sitting on my desk the day I started, giving me clear insight into the techniques that needed to be developed and the issues that needed tackling. This allowed me to implement much needed changes rapidly, with minimum time spent "getting up to speed." The fact that these changes had the approval of an outside "expert" also greatly helped me overcome the inevitable internal resistance.

Indeed, the combination of the powerful impact of an authority from outside your organisation, giving unbiased and respected professional opinions, and the weight of the arguments that make up that authority's recommendations, is at the heart of a consultant's ability to help staff effect important and far-reaching changes in organisations.

The word "recommendation" is crucial because it also illustrates the weakness felt by consultants. They can recommend but they cannot implement. They can be the best-known, most expensive and highest-performing consultancy, but their recommendations will be a waste of time and money if the organisation does not implement them. The will to implement is the key to successful consultancy and to improvements that move your organisation rapidly forward.

Reviewer's Comment

The importance of acceptance by the Board of an organisation before, during and after a consultant's visit cannot be overestimated. This may make all the difference to the successful implementation of a fundraising programme.

WHEN YOU NEED A CONSULTANT

Hiring a consultant can be seen as a two-stage process. The first is to identify that a consultant is required and to convince the appropriate people within the organisation that this is true; the second is to do the necessary preparation within the organisation before the consultant starts work, to ensure that work goes smoothly.

How do you know that a problem requires a consultant? Sometimes a consultant is required to solve an internal problem that cannot be handled by current staff or volunteers because there is a crisis. In a crisis, new solutions become possible for problems that may have been dormant and ignored for a long time. At other times, an organisation's staff may recognise that assistance is needed with an issue because they lack the necessary internal skills.

You may also need a consultant when:

■ You are planning changes to move your organisation into a new field of operation, in which you have insufficient knowledge to be confident of a successful outcome.

■ There are problems in the organisation that require experienced help in sorting them out.

■ You need interim help to fill needs in staffing.

■ The consultant can undertake key tasks that internal staff cannot or don't have time to do.

■ The consultant can assist staff or volunteers in certain tasks, such as asking for funds.

It is not uncommon for organisations to be forced by crises to seek help from a consultant. This is particularly true in fundraising, which is often undervalued and under-resourced, leading to poor performance or panic when a major source of funds comes to an end. The consultant then has to work against the clock to maximise income in a short time and safeguard the programme; but, in doing this, to also keep an eye on the longer-term sustainability of the fundraising programme. There is little point to an intervention if the recommendations only result in a series of crises, as funds periodically run out.

Sustainability usually requires investment. A consultant can help you understand the scale of that investment, can argue the case for that expenditure

Continues on next page

within your organisation, and can show how best to implement the programme, as well as measure and monitor it.

In certain circumstances, a consultant can undertake implementation of his or her recommendations by actually working within the organisation. Two specific examples are interim management and employee cover. Though it could be argued that these are not strictly consultancy functions, many consultants do undertake these roles. In other cases, consultants become operational and plug gaps in staffing or undertake key tasks. Even when it becomes obvious that a problem has not been addressed internally – and cannot be – there may be resistance within the organisation to hiring a consultant. Showing a set of consultants' credentials to those whose support you need may help them see what could be done by outside help. This is preferable to a theoretical discussion about using a consultant, particularly when arguments tend to centre on the perceived cost of the consultancy or the value of the solution.

This is the key to explaining the worth of a consultancy. Set out the outcome you expect and the benefits of that outcome.

This will give value to the exercise. Be prepared to explain, without underestimating your own or others' abilities, why the solutions will not be reached by internal staff or volunteers. Often the cost of using current staff to solve the problem is overlooked, in that they must stop activities at which they are expert in order to concentrate on activities they may not be able to handle effectively. Remember that good consultants will be passing on much of their skills to the people they work with, and this can be a strong selling point.

If in doubt about your organisation's needs, do talk it through with a consultant. Much helpful advice can come from a quick phone call; you might be surprised at the flexibility and knowledge of consultants, who have most probably encountered a very similar problem in the past.

Reviewer's Comment
It is often a good strategy to have the preferred consultant address the Board in advance of being hired. This will generally raise the level of confidence in the decision to appoint.

WHAT A CONSULTANT CAN AND CANNOT DO FOR YOU

A consultant cannot implement the changes you wish to make. In other words, he or she cannot do your job for you.

Understanding this is at the heart of understanding how a successful consultancy operation will work. The consultant brings his or her experience to bear on the problem, suggests ways to solve it and hands it to you to solve. Good consultants will have a practical as well as a theoretical understanding of the problem. They not only will have undertaken this kind of work themselves as practitioners, but also will have taken other organisations through the operation.

Good consultants can talk through their solutions effectively; that is, they ensure that you understand the issues involved in implementation, and they can convince key staff to allocate the resources necessary for the changes. It is important that consultants are given access to those who will make the decision to proceed with their recommendations. This may be at the Board or CEO level, or further down the chain of command as appropriate for the level of resources required.

Skills are transferable across national borders and across different types of not-for-profit organisations (NPOs). NPOs, internationally, have distinct structures, operations and problems, which are well understood by consultants specialising in NPOs. Cultural differences can be a stumbling block to solutions based on experience elsewhere, but culture must not be confused with tradition. Traditions can and do change; indeed, a key part of consultancy is often to challenge an organisation's traditions where these are based merely on repeating past actions rather than rising to new challenges.

Management and fundraising techniques, with few exceptions, apply across NPO fields. A good consultant who has not worked in your field will still be able to provide powerful insights and suggest effective practices.

Reputable consultants belong to a professional institute and are usually listed on that institute's website. They also advertise extensively in the trade press, speak at conferences, and mail their proposals and offers to NPOs.

Having said that, there are many countries where the NPO field does not have the usual marketing routes for consultants. NPOs are therefore advised to map the field for prospective consultants and to speak to at least three before settling on the right one for them.

The Internet is always a good place to start. Use one of the well-known search engines to find fundraising, charity or nonprofit sites within your country or region.

The other key sources of information are colleagues and friends in the field, other NPOs in your country and your key donors. A few phone calls should establish a list of possibilities. Naturally, a recommendation from another NPO, which successfully used a consultant and would employ that consultant again, is a powerful indication of the consultant's potential value to you.

Even if you do not yet need consultants, it is worthwhile taking the time to meet them at conferences or other venues where they are speaking or have a stall, and to chat to them to get information and learn about the way they operate. Adding their business cards to your collection may in time prove a very valuable investment, especially if you should ever decide to join a consultancy yourself.

O nce you have decided that hiring a consultant is the right way to go forward, it is important to set up a selection process designed to hire the best agency or person for your particular needs.

One way of selecting consultants is to ask them to make a pitch, that is to sell their services to you based on information you provide about the need you are addressing. Usually this will be in the form of demonstrating to you how well they have filled past briefs from clients and the process by which they would fulfil your needs. This method has the problem that they can only give a superficial response because they won't know your organisation very well and can only base their comments on what you write in the brief you provide.

Interviews, on the other hand, are more interactive and should be much like those you use to hire your staff. Think about the "person specific" experience and qualifications you would expect to find. Are these desirable or essential? Devise a set of questions designed to help determine if the consultants fulfil your criteria. Ask each consultant the same set of questions from a written sheet, on which you can score the answers on a scale of, say, 1 to 10 points. This will give

you a clearer indication than relying on "instinct," which can be terribly misleading.

There are many standard questions you can ask:

- Have they tackled a similar problem in the past?
- Are they associated with any professional organisations?
- In what way are they qualified?
- Who would you actually be working with – the person at the interview or a junior associate?
- Who are their other clients?

Do, of course, ask if they have worked in your country or your field before, but don't forget the transferability of consultancy skills.

When you have decided to employ a particular consultant, do ask for, and then check, his or her references.

Reviewer's Comment
Reference checking is often the only tool which can be used with certainty and objectivity when retaining a consultant. Do not underestimate its importance.

EXPECTATIONS

Managing expectations and maintaining communication are crucial to a successful relationship. Where relationships between consultants and NPOs go wrong is often in the expectations. NPOs expect too much too quickly of consultants. Consultants expect NPOs to accept their recommendations without question and implement them directly.

The consultant's fees may be a source of friction. The fees are inevitably much higher per day than the earnings of staff members whom the consultants will work with, and often much higher than the earnings of the CEO. Consultancies are, after all, for-profit organisations with all the attendant costs, no matter how much individual consultants may empathise with your mission and programme.

The consultant must make clear and the NPO understand the actual number of days needed to complete a project or a half-finished job will result.

Set out working practices to which the consultant and organisation will be accountable. (See the following example.)

The consultancy will be accountable for:

■ Adherence to agreed deadlines.

■ All its administrative and office costs.

■ Monthly progress reports.

■ Monthly billing in arrears.

The NPO will be accountable for:

■ Access to key individuals on mutually agreeable dates.

■ Provision of all information having a bearing on the project.

■ Payment in accordance with the terms and conditions.

■ Making contact with interviewees as required.

The consultancy and NPO will jointly:

■ Alert each other to anything that may materially affect the outcome of the project.

■ Respect confidentiality and all proprietary materials and approaches.

Good communication between the consultant and NPO is crucial in order to avoid problems.

Reviewer's Comment
A good and professional consultant will ensure that, after his or her departure, the relationship between the NPO and its constituency remains in good order.

HIRING THE CONSULTANT

Having determined you need a consultant, researched those appropriate to help you with your issue, interviewed them or listened to their pitches, contacted references and decided on the person or company you want to engage, you then need to go through the formal process of hiring the consultant.

If choosing the consultant has been a long process, it may be worthwhile to meet him or her again and go over the points that will form the basis of your contract – precisely what the consultant will do, how long this will take, and how much will be charged and on what basis. You should know who the actual consultant will be or who will comprise the consultancy team, and the consultant or consultancy team should know to whom they will report within your organisation. Also, how will you communicate when neither you nor the consultant is in the office?

If you have made your decision, phone them and arrange for a contract to be drawn up, if required. An exchange of letters or emails may be sufficient if the engagement is only for a short period. Do arrange the first meeting with them when you make this call so that time does not drift.

Do not forget to call all the unsuccessful consultants promptly and let them know whom you have chosen. It is useful for them to have feedback that may allow them to improve. Clear reasons are much more helpful to them than a laboured explanation or long discussion.

No matter how brief or how extensive the consultancy, you should put into writing at least the following:

■ The work you require the consultant to undertake.

■ The time frame for carrying out this work.

■ The cost and the payment schedule (e.g., monthly in arrears).

■ The notice period to end the arrangement.

■ A note of the areas the consultant should keep confidential.

■ Any legal requirements the consultant must fulfil, such as copyright and data protection.

■ A note of the schedule of any meetings and reports.

■ The law under which any dispute will be settled.

Continues on next page

Being explicit at this stage is most important because it gives each party the chance to settle any misunderstandings and to be clear about expectations. This, together with the practices described previously, should ensure both parties are quite clear about what is expected.

For a long consultancy, a complex or high-value one, a formal contract should be prepared. It may be a standard contract for consultants and other agencies which can be adapted to suit your needs or be one prepared specifically for this piece of work. Many consultancy firms have their own standard contract which will cover the key points of the relationship; however, always get legal advice on the wording before signing.

It is usual for two copies of the contract to be produced. One party signs and sends the copies to the other party who, in turn, signs both copies but only posts one back to the originator.

Consultancy is, by its nature, a short-term exercise. For consultancies of only a few days, it may not be worthwhile to create a lengthy agreement, but the terms under which the parties operate should at least be set out in a letter or email.

The first days of the consultancy are vital and usually involve introductions to key players and those the consultant will be working with on an everyday basis. The introductions will often be with people who have not been part of the hiring process, so do ensure they understand the need and work the consultant will be carrying out. Often the arrival of a consultant will mean extra work or a feeling of lowered status if the consultant is working on a long-standing problem in their department. Discussion with those staff members or volunteers is essential well before the consultant arrives.

Reviewer's Comment
Not all those within the NPO, with whom the consultant comes into contact, will have a clear understanding of just why the consultant is there. An effective consultant will ensure there is no ambiguity.

Managing the Consultancy

Once the consultant is hired, the relationship with him or her needs to be carefully managed in order to ensure the organisation receives the best work from the consultant and the consultant is able to fully utilise his or her skills on behalf of the organisation. Two important ways of ensuring this happens are regular meetings to discuss the progress of the work and reports by which the consultant keeps the organisation informed of his or her activities.

Consultants usually juggle meetings with clients and meetings with prospective new clients in a complicated diary, which can change from day to day. Do set a schedule for regular weekly or monthly management meetings with the consultants, depending on the appropriate time frame, and let them know that you expect these meetings to be kept.

The purpose of these meetings is to keep track of the work against the targets originally set, to have time to talk about any small problems before they grow into large ones, and to look at the next work period to ensure circumstances have not necessitated changes. They can also be used to discuss any other problems that the organisation may be facing. These discussions may also show where the consultant can assist in the future. Indeed, consultants say that most of their work comes from new business for existing clients and from word of mouth when those clients pass their names on to colleagues in other organisations.

Like regular meetings, regular reports keep the work on track and expectations in order. For short consultancy periods, there may only be one report at the end of the consultancy; for others, there may be a series of monthly reports. These should not be too detailed or you will be paying for report writing, not consulting, but they should give you a clear picture of whether the work is meeting your schedule and targets.

In real life, things change unexpectedly. It would be odd if nothing arose to alter the schedule or the targets, but it is good to learn about changes as soon as possible. Putting things in writing covers both sides in case of any disagreements and tends to dissipate wishful thinking about outcomes or timetables.

An alternative to formal reports is to write minutes of the monthly meetings and ensure they are circulated; that way, any critical problems will be brought up quickly, rather than being left to be corrected at the next meeting.

When things go well, an organisation should tell all of those involved. A call to the consultant to say "thank you" or a brief note can be very motivating and help keep things moving.

Each consultant will have favourite clients who make working with them a pleasure. These clients are usually engaged in dealing with the problem being addressed, are passionate about the organisation, respond quickly to queries, and are personable with the consultant. These clients bring out the best in the consultant and are likely to find the consultant going the extra mile for their organisation.

The difficult clients are those for whom nothing is ever quite right, and minor points are treated as major disasters. These clients tend not to work with the consultant; instead, they stand aside and look critically at the consultant's work, expecting miracles.

So if you have a good working relationship with consultants, look at other areas where they may be able to assist you. Recommend them to your colleagues and keep the relationship going. Do not leave the consultants to continue in their work alone.

In a consultancy lasting over a long period of time, the momentum of the work needs continual maintenance through each phase. For example, in a capital appeal, there is likely to be an initial feasibility study, then a private phase when the consultant works with the organisation and its major donors before the appeal is publicly launched, and then the public phase when the organisation makes the appeal. Each is radically different and requires a different relationship between the consultant and organisation.

Just like any partnership, good relationships need to be maintained by hard work, open lines of communication and recognition that as needs shift, everyone must be flexible in order to achieve the results set out in the original engagement of the consultant.

WHEN THINGS GO BADLY

When things go badly, any suppressed internal resentments about the use of a consultant may surface, making a rational decision hard to reach. The first step is to stop and acknowledge that there is a problem (always best done early, face to face, before the problem grows), then to specify the nature of the problem. Is this a failure to reach a financial target or a failure of communication? ("We didn't know you were going to do that.") Is it a failure of the relationship ("Why are you treating us like this?") or another problem? Once the problem is defined, the second step is to look for constructive steps forward. "We would like you to do this in the future" is more helpful than "Why did you do that?" But you may first want to know why an action was or was not taken. The result may surprise you.

Of course, no client should tolerate shoddy work or poor performance. A consultant who constantly cancels meetings, doesn't work according to the agreed processes, or is obviously more interested in other clients needs to be quickly reminded of his or her responsibilities. If the consultant has no satisfactory reply, the consultancy should be terminated as soon as possible. See if there is action you can take under the contract or if there are recommendations by any professional organisation's Code of Practice. You can refer serious problems to the standard-setting body in the industry and follow its complaints procedure. Consultants' reputations are very valuable commodities, which they risk losing at their own peril.

Naturally, before you take these steps, you should ensure that you are faced with a real problem caused by the consultant's actions and not simply the unrealistic expectations of people within the organisation.

Reviewer's Comment
In some instances, a change in personnel from the consultancy at the NPO site can make all the difference to the successful completion of the task.

Having consultants work for your organisation provides a number of collateral possibilities in addition to the actual work which they are engaged to perform.

Do these things:

- Pick their brains and learn all you can from them, so that you don't need to hire another consultant in that area again.

- Think about how they operate – chairing meetings, giving presentations, analysing problems, deriving solutions – and try these techniques out in your daily work.

- Think about how they interact with other staff. They often need to pick up information, inspire confidence and win support for their ideas quite quickly.

- Think about their dress, manner and how they have impact. Where does their authority come from when they are not part of the management structure?

- Talk to them about other parts of your work that may be troubling you. They may have some very good ideas.

- Many people know what they should do but cannot implement their ideas. What processes does your consultant suggest?

- Use them as bridges. Do your consultants have contacts or colleagues who could help you? Do they know influential people, or can they point you to others who can assist?

Crucially: Actively manage the entire process with the consultant. Agree on the work, check that it is being carried out, praise good work, and discuss poor performance.

Reviewer's Comment
Good consultants ensure key skills and competencies remain with the NPO after their departure. They see this as part of their responsibility to the client.

MENTORING

Mentoring is a great way to use a consultant. Here, the consultant usually spends a minimum of time but brings expertise and experience to a member of staff who is new to his or her work or to a specific task. The staff member's ability to undertake that work at a high level is greatly enhanced, and he or she learns exactly how the task should be approached and carried out.

Mentoring is not only for junior staff, who need to update their skills or acquire new skills, but also for senior management. At the senior level, mentoring is very useful in many ways. For example, a director experienced in communication may need to develop fundraising skills or an understanding of finance, including reading and preparing a balance sheet and profit and loss account. It is also useful to help develop interpersonal skills, presentations, public speaking, personal grooming, and all those other skills that suddenly acquire much greater significance than they had in the director's previous position.

In general, mentoring is a process of passing on skills rather than solving a single problem or set of problems. It is usually a long-term process, though with only a few days per month involved.

Reviewer's Comment
Essential parts of a successful consultancy will be advice and recommendations regarding continuing professional development for relevant employees of the NPO.

INTERIM MANAGEMENT

Recruiting staff doesn't always go smoothly. Suitable candidates may not be available, or that prize catch might decline your offer, having been seduced by greener organisational pastures elsewhere. Any one of a hundred unforeseen problems might forestall the recruitment process, and your organisation becomes left with a gap in management.

This may be a time when you could hire a consultant – particularly one who has specific skills that fit the job or one who knows your organisation – to fill the gap and keep your projects on track. Some top managers only work as consultants who take roles in interim management, finding the variety stimulating, the pay good and the flexibility challenging. Most consultants can undertake interim management in their own field and often prove very effective. This is sometimes because they are released from the everyday world of internal politics, and carry the authority and experience to implement tasks and see them through.

As with any consultancy relationship, one key to success is getting the brief right. Both parties need to know exactly what the consultant is expected to do and what the consultant is expected to achieve. Is this person going to achieve any specific goals while he or she is in the management position, or is the consultant merely holding the fort and keeping staff working to schedule?

Change Management

A key potential use of consultants, often overlooked by NPOs, is having them help with undertaking change in the organisation. There are, for example, several stages that NPOs move through during their growth from start-ups to mature organisations. Each of these stages involves a degree of upheaval, and the advice of an outsider can minimise the problems and develop clear solutions.

If an organisation has grown to the stage where the director can no longer effectively manage each member of staff directly, the organisation may need to move into a divisional structure. Agreeing on the responsibility for those divisions, talking staff through their personal changes (many will feel a loss of status as they no longer report to the director), and setting a timetable for recruiting divisional heads, writing job descriptions, etc., can all be enhanced by tapping into the experience of a consultant who has undertaken this work before or assisted another organisation through these changes.

Similarly, when a major project lasting, say, three years is started, it may require radical change in the organisation and new ways of working, perhaps including precise monitoring and evaluation to a degree with which the organisation is not familiar. Setting the project structure, policies and practices may be best undertaken with the advice of a consultant.

Another key change is when two organisations merge or when a division is split off to form a separate organisation. Likewise, the creation of a for-profit company to support a charity, or the creation of a charitable wing for a for-profit organisation, may benefit from outside advice and assistance.

Change management requires close cooperation between the organisation and the consultant. It is possible that people will be upset and find fault with the consultant or other change leader. Therefore, the process for change should be one which is based on consultation, with adequate time taken to air and understand diverse views. The process should also be clear to everyone and then move forward with definite decisions and conclusions.

FUNDRAISING

undraising consultants can provide a range of advice to an organisation. They may provide change, or interim, management or just advice on raising funds from certain sources, such as trusts or foundations or major donors.

Fundraising consultants are often asked to raise money in return for a percentage of the funds raised. The guidelines set out by fundraising bodies do not support this practice. Individuals and agencies do not want to see a percentage of their donations going to consultants. Also, it is often impossible at the end of the day to determine who was responsible for raising the funds. Once the funds are raised, NPOs may lose interest in paying the consultants, and good consultants will not engage in this practice.

Fundraising consultants may, however, be closely involved in raising funds by devising a fundraising programme, helping with writing letters and other copy, designing and sending out fundraising materials on behalf of the NPO, or by otherwise engaging in the fundraising process. Of course, they also advise and train staff to do this.

Fundraising consultants do not come with attached sources of funds or major donors who give because of their advice. The consultant is usually invisible to the donor, working through the NPO; this way, the NPO presents the best case to the donor, whether an individual person or a funding agency.

Often fundraising consultants work on those areas of fundraising that NPOs do not have occasion to undertake very often, such as capital appeals, high-level applications to international bodies, or major-donor fundraising. In these cases, using a consultant is often imperative. The work demands specialist knowledge that is unlike any other part of the fundraising operation, and a common-sense approach is often just not good enough to raise the needed funds. If the fundraising programmes have any problems, the NPO will usually not be able to repeat the work. If a capital appeal or major-donor programme offends people or fails to reach its target, it is often impossible to go back and ask for more money from the same sources. If an application does not succeed, you may not be able to apply again until the following year, and may then have to overcome a bad first impression.

Fundraising consultants are often best used to set the fundraising strategy in the early days of fundraising; instead, they are sometimes brought in when there is a crisis in the fundraising, and income is needed quickly to prop-up the organisation's services. Naturally, this is the most difficult time to release extra money to fuel the fundraising process, but that may be just what is needed. Indeed, a consultant can ensure that these funds are spent wisely and are adequate to secure their goal. A good consultant will also advise how the organisation can best avoid future falls in income.

Reviewer's Comment

In general terms, consultants bring no authority to the table among the constituents of the NPO with whom they are working. By definition, this significantly lessens their possible effectiveness in the asking process.

Governance

The effectiveness or ineffectiveness of an organisation is often set at the Board (or council) level by the voluntary trustees and directors who set policy for the organisation. When NPOs are small, these volunteers often carry out practical work for the organisation; as the organisation grows, they usually take a more distant role as policy makers and overseers of staff.

This transition and many other problems of governance can often be greatly helped by consultants because they are seen as neutral and are experienced in the governance and management of a wide variety of organisations, from which they draw useful ways of working to achieve organisational goals.

Personalities sometimes play a deciding role here, and the help of an experienced professional can often unlock solutions that would be impossible for insiders to tackle effectively.

Governance is so important that it is worthwhile for an organisation to review it periodically. A consultant can greatly enhance this process, giving it an edge not found in the usual process of trustees or directors taking a day together off-site to discuss various issues.

The relationship between the governing body and the chief executive is one which, when it goes sour, often leads to very serious problems. In this situation, a consultant can apply professional criteria which are separate from the internal politics of the situation. Roles, territory, and the formal and informal ways of working together can all come under professional scrutiny.

CONCLUSION

Using consultants is an exceptionally effective way of moving an organisation forward into new territory or solving contentious internal problems. The whole procedure, however, requires active management from start to finish.

The answers to the following questions will remind you of the key elements in choosing and using consultants.

- Have you considered the variety of ways in which a consultant can help?

- Do you have internal agreement to hire a consultant?

- Are you talking to the right consultants, experienced in finding solutions to your type of problem, even if they have not previously worked in your field or country?

- Have you set out the processes in terms of reporting, meetings, invoicing, etc.?

- Have you agreed on the schedule of work and what should happen by when? This may need to be developed, or finalised, once the consultants have spent time with the organisation.

- Once the work starts, are you meeting regularly with the consultants and tackling any problems as they occur?

- Do you need to extend the consultancy to include help with implementation?

- Now that you know the consultants, can they tackle any other problems?

Always balance use of a consultant against other possibilities, and be prepared to argue your case for or against. Once you decide to use consultants, take the time to be professional in managing the project.

Remember that the largest commercial companies use consultants – it is a sign of strength, not weakness.

DR. JOHN BAGULEY, BA (HONS), MBA, MIoF

John Baguley is an experienced management and fundraising consultant and is director of the International Fundraising Consultancy, which is based in the UK with partner agencies worldwide. (See www.ifc.tc.) He is the author of *Successful Fundraising*, a comprehensive guide to fundraising published by Bibliotek Books in English. He has written extensively on fundraising, and has lectured and worked in all parts of the world.

John is a former fundraising director at Amnesty International UK, Friends of the Earth and the Medical Foundation. He has worked for Oxfam and other international development organisations. He has also served on the Board of various NPOs.

John was the first director of international fundraising for Amnesty's International Secretariat and the first director of the Soil Association. He has extensive overseas experience and has just completed a doctorate in the international development of NGOs.

John has lectured at fundraising workshops in the UK, Holland, India, Nepal, the Philippines, Hong Kong, Taiwan, Ukraine, and Kazakhstan. He has helped organisations raise funds in the U.S., South America, Africa, Asia, Eastern Europe, Central Asia and Western Europe.

Frank Opray, Reviewer

Frank Opray, has ten years' experience as director of development, first at Wesley College Melbourne and subsequently at Carey Grammar School Melbourne.

Prior to these appointments he spent many years in finance, market research and management consulting, primarily in the services sector. During that time he was for three years a Council member and Treasurer of Wesley College Melbourne, Australia's largest school with more than 3,600 students.

In recognition of his work in fundraising and marketing at Wesley and for the development profession, Frank received the inaugural award of "Fundraiser of the Year" at the 1992 joint conference of the Australian Institute of Fundraising and the Association of Development and Alumni Professionals in Education (ADAPE).

Frank regularly presents papers at educational conferences in Australia, Asia and Europe.